# WYOMING

## Laura Pratt

www.av2books.com

Go to **www.av2books.com,**
and enter this book's
unique code.

## BOOK CODE

**P839432**

**AV² by Weigl** brings you media
enhanced books that support
active learning.

AV² provides enriched content that supplements and complements this book. Weigl's AV² books
strive to create inspired learning and engage young minds in a total learning experience.

# Your AV² Media Enhanced books come alive with...

**Audio**
Listen to sections of
the book read aloud.

**Video**
Watch informative
video clips.

**Embedded Weblinks**
Gain additional information
for research.

**Try This!**
Complete activities and
hands-on experiments.

**Key Words**
Study vocabulary, and
complete a matching
word activity.

**Quizzes**
Test your knowledge.

**Slide Show**
View images and
captions, and prepare
a presentation.

# ... and much, much more!

Published by AV² by Weigl
350 5ᵗʰ Avenue, 59ᵗʰ Floor
New York, NY  10118
Website: www.av2books.com          www.weigl.com

Library of Congress Cataloging-in-Publication Data
Pratt, Laura.
 Wyoming / by Laura Pratt.
    p. cm. -- (Explore the U.S.A.)
 Includes bibliographical references and index.
 ISBN 978-1-61913-421-8 (hard cover : alk. paper)
 1.  Wyoming--Juvenile literature.  I. Title.
 F761.3.P72 2013
 978.7--dc23
                              2012018260

Printed in the United States of America in North Mankato, Minnesota
1 2 3 4 5 6 7 8 9  16 15 14 13 12

052012
WEP040512

**Project Coordinator:** Karen Durrie
**Art Director:** Terry Paulhus

Weigl acknowledges Getty Images as the primary image supplier
for this title. Page 16 train photo courtesy Philip J Zocco.

# WYOMING

## Contents

2 AV² Book Code
4 Nickname
6 Location
8 History
10 Flower and Seal
12 Flag
14 Animal
16 Capital
18 Goods
20 Fun Things to Do
22 Facts
24 Key Words

3

This is Wyoming.
It is called the Equality State.
Wyoming was the first state
where women could vote.

This is the shape of Wyoming. It is in the north part of the United States.

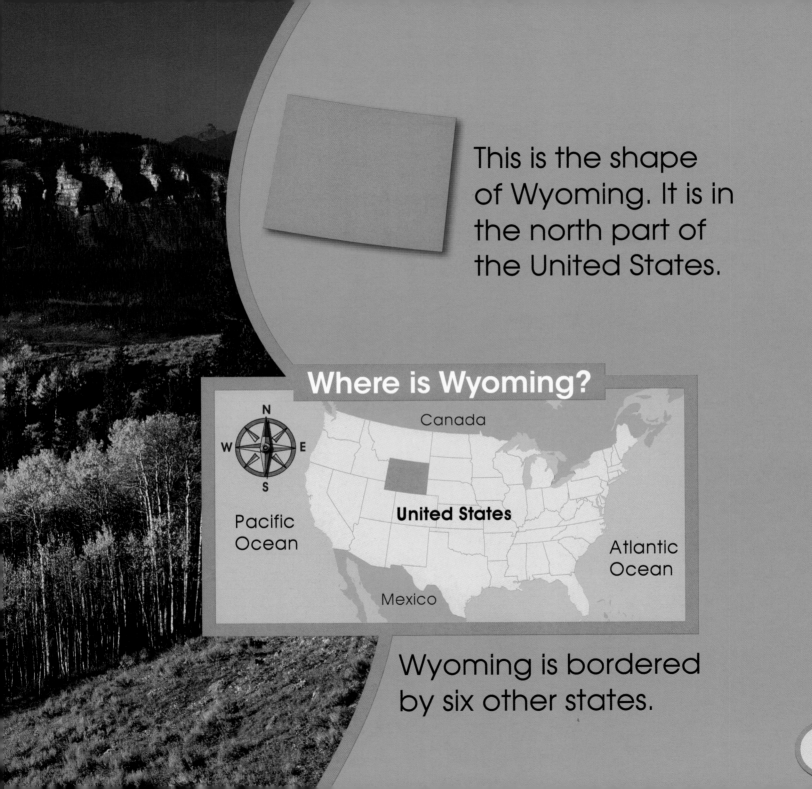

## Where is Wyoming?

Canada

Pacific Ocean

United States

Atlantic Ocean

Mexico

Wyoming is bordered by six other states.

Wyoming has a rodeo called Cheyenne Frontier Days. The rodeo is 116 years old. It started with ranch cowboys having a bucking horse contest.

Cheyenne Frontier Days is the largest outdoor rodeo in the country.

The Indian paintbrush is the Wyoming state flower. It looks like it has been dipped in red paint.

The Wyoming state seal has a woman, a farmer, and a miner.

The seal also has an eagle at the bottom.

This is the state flag of Wyoming. It has a bison in the middle. The flag is red, white, and blue.

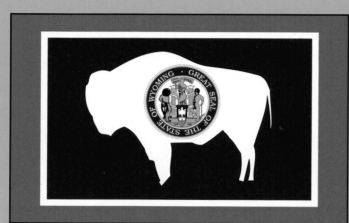

The state seal is on the bison.

The state animal of Wyoming is the bison. The bison is the heaviest land animal in the United States.

A bison can weigh up to 2,200 pounds.

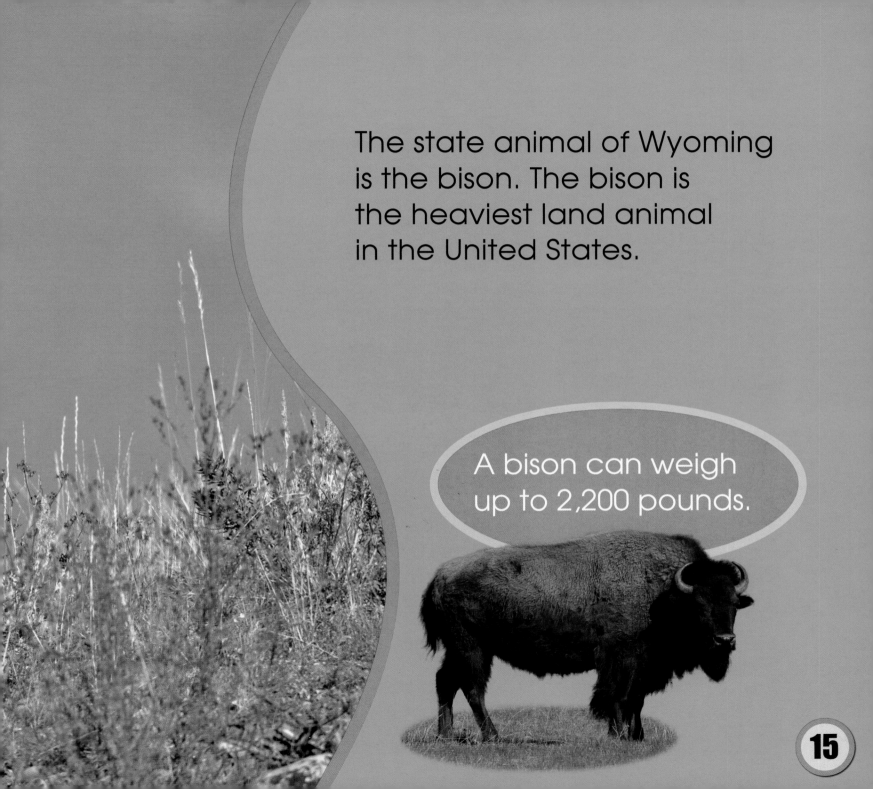

This is the biggest city in Wyoming. It is named Cheyenne. It is the state capital.

Cheyenne has the largest steam train in the world.

Wyoming has sheep. Wool is made from sheep fleece. Wyoming makes more than $6 million each year from wool.

More than 412,000 sheep live in Wyoming.

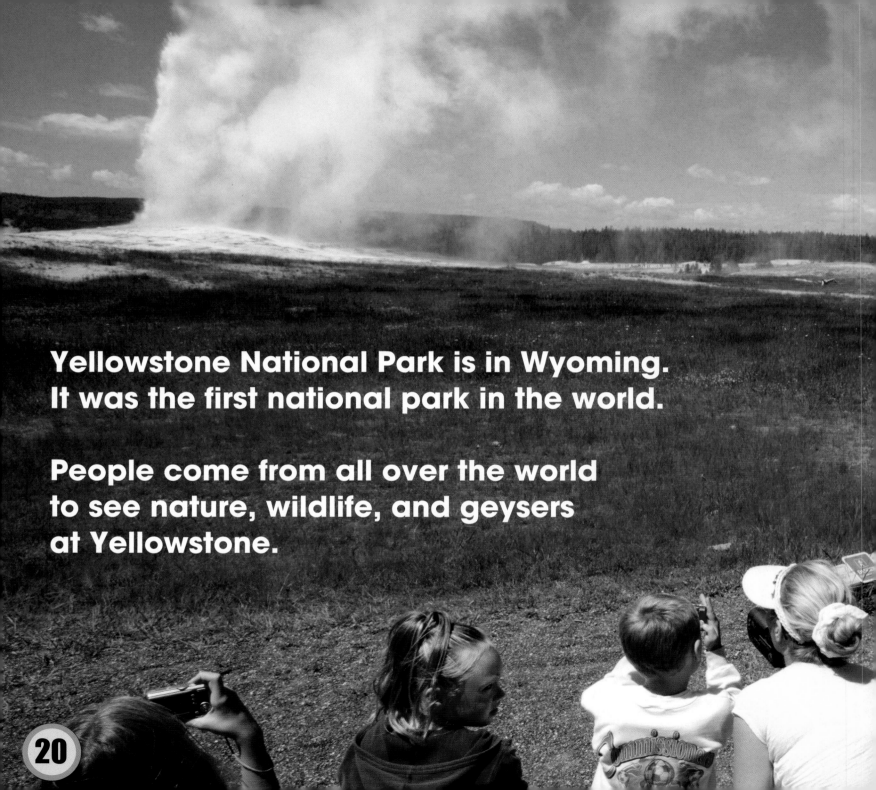

Yellowstone National Park is in Wyoming.
It was the first national park in the world.

People come from all over the world
to see nature, wildlife, and geysers
at Yellowstone.

# WYOMING FACTS

These pages provide detailed information that expands on the interesting facts found in the book. These pages are intended to be used by adults as a learning support to help young readers round out their knowledge of each state in the *Explore the U.S.A.* series.

**Pages 4–5**

Wyoming was the first state to allow women to vote in political elections. Wyoming's first territorial governor, John A. Campbell, signed a bill on December 10, 1869, granting women this right. Wyoming had the first female justice of the peace in the United States, the first female juror, and was the first to elect a female governor.

**Pages 6–7**

On July 10, 1890, Wyoming joined the United States as the 44th state. The state borders Montana, South Dakota, Nebraska, Colorado, Utah, and Idaho. Wyoming has many mountain ranges. The Big Horn Mountains, Rocky Mountains, Black Hills, Grand Tetons, and Sierra Madre ranges all rise up out of Wyoming.

**Pages 8–9**

Cheyenne Frontier Days has been held outdoors since 1897. Wyoming cowboys used to hold bronc riding contests on area ranches. Other cowboys began to travel to Cheyenne to compete. Today, top rodeo competitors compete to win more than $1 million dollars. Cheyenne Frontier Days runs for 10 days each July.

**Pages 10–11**

The Indian paintbrush is also called the desert paintbrush. This plant is known for its bright colors, which can vary from orange to scarlet to purple. The state seal features a woman standing in front of a banner that says "Equal Rights." Banners on the pillars beside the woman list items important to the Wyoming economy, including oil, mines, livestock, and grain.

**Pages 12–13**

The flag of Wyoming shows a bison with the state seal in the center. The bison is shown facing away from the flagpole to symbolize the freedom bison once had in the state. The eagle and shield represent Wyoming's support for the United States.

**Pages 14–15**

A male bison can stand up to 6 feet (1.8 meters) tall. Bison were very important to American Indians. Tens of millions of bison once roamed across in the Wyoming region. When European settlers arrived in the late 1800s, bison were hunted almost to extinction. Wyoming is one of only six states that has wild bison.

**Pages 16–17**

Cheyenne is located in the geographic center of North America. The name *Cheyenne* comes from a Sioux Indian word that means "people of alien speech." Cheyenne is often windy. There are many wind farms around the state.

**Pages 18–19**

Wyoming is the second largest wool producer in the United States. One sheep can make up to 30 pounds (13.6 kilograms) of wool in one year. Wyoming sheep produce more than 3 million pounds (1.4 million kg) of wool each year. Sheep wool is spun into yarn and used to make items such as sweaters and rugs.

**Pages 20–21**

Yellowstone National Park was the first official national park in the world. The Old Faithful geyser is one of the park's most popular attractions. A geyser is a hot spring that boils up through a vent in the Earth. Old Faithful erupts every 91 minutes. Yellowstone Park has unusual landscapes and wildlife, such as grizzly bears and bison.

# KEY WORDS

Research has shown that as much as 65 percent of all written material published in English is made up of 300 words. These 300 words cannot be taught using pictures or learned by sounding them out. They must be recognized by sight. This book contains 51 common sight words to help young readers improve their reading fluency and comprehension. This book also teaches young readers several important content words, such as proper nouns. These words are paired with pictures to aid in learning and improve understanding.

| Page | Sight Words First Appearance |
|------|------------------------------|
| 4 | could, first, is, it, state, the, this, was, where |
| 7 | by, in, many, of, other, part |
| 8 | a, country, has, old, with, years |
| 11 | also, an, and, at, been, Indian, like, looks |
| 12 | on, white |
| 15 | animals, can, land, to, up |
| 16 | city, named, world |
| 19 | each, from, live, made, makes, more, than |
| 21 | all, come, over, people, see |

| Page | Content Words First Appearance |
|------|-------------------------------|
| 4 | equality, women, Wyoming |
| 7 | shape, United States |
| 8 | Cheyenne Frontier Days, contest, cowboys, horse, rodeo |
| 11 | bottom, eagle, farmer, flower, miner, paint, paintbrush, seal |
| 12 | bison, flag, middle |
| 15 | pounds |
| 16 | capital, steam train |
| 19 | fleece, sheep, wool |
| 21 | geysers, nature, wildlife, Yellowstone National Park |

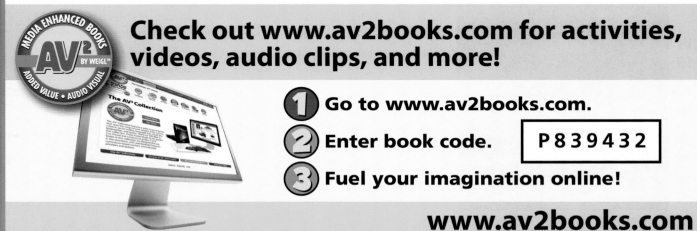